Anthology 2

T0340585

William Collins' dream of knowledge for all began with the publication of his first book in 1819. A self-educated mill worker, he not only enriched millions of lives, but also founded a flourishing publishing house. Today, staying true to this spirit, Collins books are packed with inspiration, innovation and practical expertise. They place you at the centre of a world of possibility and give you exactly what you need to explore it.

Collins. Freedom to teach.

Published by Collins
An imprint of HarperCollins*Publishers*
The News Building
1 London Bridge Street
London
SE1 9GF

HarperCollinsPublishers
Macken House, 39/40 Mayor Street Upper,
Dublin 1,
D01 C9W8,
Ireland

Browse the complete Collins catalogue at
www.collins.co.uk

© HarperCollins*Publishers* Limited 2015

15

ISBN 978-0-00-816045-6

All rights reserved. No part of this publication may be reproduced, stored in a retrieval system, or transmitted in any form or by any means, electronic, mechanical, photocopying, recording or otherwise, without the prior written permission of the Publisher or a licence permitting restricted copying in the United Kingdom issued by the Copyright Licensing Agency Ltd, 90 Tottenham Court Road, London W1T 4LP.

British Library Cataloguing in Publication Data

A Catalogue record for this publication is available from the British Library

Publishing Manager: Lizzie Catford
Project Managers: Dawn Booth and Sarah Thomas
Copy editor: Dawn Booth
Cover design and artwork: Amparo Barrera and Lynsey Murray at Davidson Publishing Solutions
Internal design: Davidson Publishing Solutions
Artwork: QBS pp.22, 23, 24, 25, 26, 27, 28, 29, 30, 54, 55, 56, 57

Acknowledgements
The publishers wish to thank the following for permission to reproduce content. Every effort has been made to trace copyright holders and to obtain their permission for the use of copyright materials. The publishers will gladly receive any information enabling them to rectify any error or omission at the first opportunity.

Extracts and illustrations on pp.6–12 from *Rapunzel* reprinted by permission of HarperCollins Publishers Ltd © 2010 Sarah Gibb; pp.13–19: *The Great Chapatti Chase* reprinted by permission of HarperCollins Publishers Ltd ©2015 Penny Dolan; An extract and 3 illustrations on pp.20–21 from *The Runaway Dinner* by Allan Ahlberg, illustrated by Bruce Ingman, Walker Books, text copyright © 2006 Allan Ahlberg, illustrations copyright © 2006 Bruce Ingman. Reproduced by permission of Walker Books Ltd, London SE11 5HJ, www.walker.co.uk; Extracts on pp.22–26 from *Tom's Sausage Lion* by Michael Morpurgo, published by HarperCollins, 2006, pp.5–6, 17–19, 66–67. Reproduced by permission of David Higham Associates Ltd; The poem on p.30 "Spin me a Web, Spider" by Charles Causley published in *I Had a Little Cat: Collected Poems for Children,* Macmillan, 2009, p.53. Reproduced by permission of David Higham Associates Ltd; The poem on p.31 "Who's There?" by Judith Nicholls, copyright © Judith Nicholls, 1990. Reproduced by kind permission of the author Judith Nicholls; Extracts and illustrations on pp.34–36 from *50 Science Things to Make and Do* by Georgina Andrews and Kate Knighton, copyright © 2008 Usborne Publishing Ltd and pp.40–41 from *Gerbils* by Laura Howell, copyright © 2005 Usborne Publishing Ltd. Reproduced by permission of Usborne Publishing, 83–85 Saffron Hill, London EC1N 8RT, UK, www.usborne.com; An extract on p.37 from *Your Senses* reprinted by permission of HarperCollins Publishers Ltd © 2012 Sally Morgan and one illustration © 2012 Maurizio De Angelis; An extract on pp. 38–39 from *Living Dinosaurs* reprinted by permission of HarperCollins Publishers Ltd ©2007 Jonathan and Angela Scott; An extract and two illustrations on pp.40–41 from *Fabulous Creatures – Are They Real?* reprinted by permission of HarperCollins Publishers Ltd © 2005 Scoular Anderson; An extract on pp.44–47 from *Diary of a Fly* reprinted by permission of HarperCollins Publishers Ltd © 2013 Doreen Cronin and five illustrations © 2012 Harry Bliss; An extract on pp.48–50 from *Diary of a Worm* reprinted by permission of HarperCollins Publishers Ltd © 2012 Doreen Cronin and four illustrations © 2003 Harry Bliss; Extracts and illustrations on pp.51–53 from *The Incredible Book Eating Boy* reprinted by permission of HarperCollins Publishers Ltd © 2006 Oliver Jeffers; Extracts on pp.54–57 from *Black Dog* by Levi Pinfold, Templar Publishing, 2012, copyright © 2011 by Levi Pinfold. Reproduced with permission of the publisher; Extracts and two illustrations on pp.58–59 from *The Day the Crayons Quit* reprinted by permission of HarperCollins Publishers Ltd © 2013 Drew Daywalt, illustrated by Oliver Jeffers; An extract and two illustrations on pp.60–61 from *Dear Greenpeace* by Simon James, Walker Books, text and illustrations, copyright © 1991 Simon James. Reproduced by permission of Walker Books Ltd, London SE11 5HJ, www.walker.co.uk; An extract on pp.62–65 from *Antarctica – Land of the Penguins* reprinted by permission of HarperCollins Publishers Ltd © 2005 Jonathan and Angela Scott; *If* on pp.66–71 reprinted by permission of HarperCollins Publishers Ltd © 2012 Mij Kelly

Photos: (t) = top; (c) = centre; (b) = bottom
pp.34, 36 © 2008 Howard Allman; pp.62, 64 Jonathan and Angela Scott

Printed and bound in the UK by Ashford Colour Press Ltd

MIX
Paper | Supporting responsible forestry
FSC
www.fsc.org
FSC™ C007454

Anthology 2

Contents

Fairy tales

From **Rapunzel** by Sarah Gibb

A young gardener and his wife were finally going to have the child they'd longed for. Sadly, the wife fell ill and the only thing that could cure her was a fresh salad picked from the enchanted garden of the witch next door. Unfortunately, the wicked witch caught the gardener picking the vegetables and demanded that, as payment, the baby be given to her. Soon after the birth, the baby was taken by the witch to a secret castle, where she grew up.

One day, the witch took Rapunzel by the hand and led her into the forest, muttering, "You're too beautiful for your own good!"

"Where are we going?" asked Rapunzel innocently as the witch led her down secret paths, deeper and deeper into the trees.

Suddenly they came to a clearing and there in the middle was a tall tower, with no door; just a few windows at the very top.

"This is your new home!" cried the witch gleefully. "No one will ever find you here, except me!"

To Rapunzel's amazement, although the tower was a slender as a tree, inside there was room after beautiful room, lit by thousands of delicate lamps which glowed as bright as day. Right at the top of the tower was a tiny balcony and Rapunzel's friends, the birds, who had followed her through the forest, gathered to greet her and eat out of her hand.

The forest creatures were sorry for the beautiful girl locked away from the world and spent many hours playing with her as she wandered from room to room in the enchanted tower.

Every morning the witch came to visit, and as there were no doors, she had worked out a special system. She would arrive at the tower and call out, "Rapunzel, Rapunzel, let down your golden hair!"

And Rapunzel would come to the edge of the tower, unfasten her glorious braid and send it tumbling down to the witch below. The old woman would nimbly scramble up the smooth side of the tower, clinging on to Rapunzel's hair as if it were a rope. Then the two would have breakfast together.

In this way several years passed until, eventually, Rapunzel began to grow bored with her prison. She had everything she could want – and yet the days seemed to pass so slowly as she sat at the top of the tower, singing sadly to herself and combing her long hair.

...

Rapunzel was both amazed and scared when the prince
appeared. But he smiled at her in such a friendly way and
he spoke so pleasantly that soon they were talking and laughing
together as if they had always known each other. The hours
flew past and all too soon it was time for the prince to slip away,
back to his palace.

...

Every morning, Rapunzel could hardly wait for the old witch to leave so that her prince could arrive. Until, one day, the witch began to watch her suspiciously, puzzled at her new-found sparkle. But Rapunzel was in another world and she didn't notice.

"It's strange," she mused dreamily, "you take so long to climb up the tower these days. The prince almost seems to **fly** up to me!"

10

The witch started in stunned horror. She could hardly
believe her ears. "**Snake!** You've betrayed me!" she
screeched. "There's no punishment good enough for you!"
In a terrible rage, she grabbed hold of a huge pair of
scissors and hacked off Rapunzel's beautiful braid, tying it
to the balcony of the tower. Then she drove Rapunzel out
into the forest, hoping that wild animals would attack her,
or that she would starve.

...

Then one morning, while he was wandering in a fog of pain, he heard a beautiful voice singing a sad song about her long-lost love. It was his Rapunzel! The forest animals had led him to her. He shouted with joy and stumbled towards the sound of her voice.

Rapunzel was horrified to see how badly hurt he was and she wept to see his poor eyes. The prince lifted his hands to touch her face. As he did so, her tears fell on his eyelids and, magically, they were healed. He could see again!

12

Traditional tales

The Great Chapatti Chase by Penny Dolan

Long ago and faraway, in a village in India, a woman walked wearily home from the well.

"And now it's time to make my bread," she said with a sigh, going into her small kitchen. She threw some handfuls of flour into a tin bowl, poured in a trickle of cool water and kneaded it all together to make some dough.

Pop! She placed a small piece between the palms of her hands. Round and round she rolled that dough, making a small round ball.

Then she placed the ball on a square wooden board, took her little rolling pin and set to work.

The woman rolled the dough flat and turned it, again and again, until she had made a perfectly round chapatti.

The woman smiled. "My, what a handsome little chapatti," she said. "You'll be delicious to eat!" And – flip, flap! – she flung that chapatti on to the hot iron stove.

However – believe it or not! – as soon as this little chapatti felt the fire, he puffed out his fat round cheeks and grinned.

"Delicious to eat?" he replied, laughing. "No, no, you silly woman! I'm not staying to be eaten!"

With that, he jumped off the stove and rolled right out of the door, singing for all to hear: "**Run, run as fast as you can! You can't catch me, I'm Chapatti Man!**"

"Come back!" the woman cried. She chased after him, with all her bangles jangling. "Come back!" called her children, running as fast as they could, but not one was swift enough to catch up with that cheeky little chapatti.

After a while, the chapatti came to a weaver's hut. A watchful cat crouched on a tall stack of carpets. As the little chapatti rolled by, she jumped down.

"Stop, stop! You look good to eat!" she mewed.

"Eat me, you fluffy fleabag? No, no!" the little chapatti answered. He rolled right out of the yard, singing:

"**Run, run as fast as you can. You can't catch me, I'm Chapatti Man!**"

The cat raced after him, her fur all in a frizz, but she was just not fast enough.

Before long, the chapatti came to a busy market. A dog lay dozing under a stall. As the little chapatti rolled by, he leapt up, tail wagging with excitement.

14

"Stop, stop! You look good to eat!" he yelped.

"Huh! Do you think I'd let myself be eaten by a silly dog like you?" the little chapatti answered, rolling right past, and singing: **"Run, run as fast as you can. You can't catch me, I'm Chapatti Man!"**

The dog ran, barking, after the runaway, but soon he gave up too.

On down the road rolled that little chapatti.

After a while, he came across an elderly goat, nibbling the grass by the roadside. She stopped chewing when she saw the little chapatti rolling by.

"Stop, stop! You look good to eat!" she bleated. "Come here!"

"No way!" You're not nibbling me, you giddy goat!" laughed the little chapatti. He rolled right past her, singing: **"Run, run as fast as you can! You can't catch me, I'm Chapatti Man!"**

The goat tried trotting after him, but the long halter round her neck held her back.

On rolled the little chapatti man, chuckling to himself.

A brown cow came wandering along the road. She stared as the little chapatti came rolling towards her.

"Stop, stop, you look good to eat!" she mooed.

"No, no! Why should I be munched up by you, you lazy lump?" the little chapatti answered and away he rolled, singing: "**Run, run as fast as you can. You can't catch me, I'm Chapatti Man!**"

The cow charged after him, with the bell on her collar clanging loudly. Quite soon, she grew weary, and sat herself down by the road to rest.

Eventually, the little chapatti rolled towards a fine country house. A magnificent elephant was waiting outside, ready for a procession.

"Stop, stop, you look good to eat!" the elephant trumpeted, raising her trunk and flapping her big ears.

"I'm not stopping for you, big fancy face!" called the little chapatti, chuckling.

He rolled right on, singing: "**Run, run as fast as you can. You can't catch me, I'm Chapatti Man!**"

The elephant ran after him, with all her ornaments swaying, and all the people shouting, but soon even she came to a halt.

The little chapatti rolled on and on into a forest. After a while, the path led him down to the banks of a wide river.

"Bother, bother!" How can I get across?" he cried. "I don't want to end up soggy and wet."

"You poor thing!" purred a soft voice. "Maybe I can help you?"

The little chapatti looked up and saw a handsome tiger stretched out along the branch of a tree.

The tiger yawned, clambered lazily down, and gave an enormous smile.

"Little Chapatti Man, I can't bear to see you in trouble. If you sat on my tail. I could carry you across the water," he said. "Tigers are very good at swimming."

"Thank you, dear, kind Tiger!" cried the little chapatti. Without a thought, he jumped – flip flap! – on to the tiger's tail.

17

Tiger swam seven strokes, but gradually his striped tail began to droop.

"Help! The water is closer," squeaked the little chapatti.

"Sorry, little Chapatti Man. My tail feels rather tired today. Why don't you roll up on to my back?"

So the chapatti did just that.

When Tiger reached the middle of the river, he swam so very slowly that the water lapped against his furry sides.

"Take care, Tiger! The water is even closer," squealed the little chapatti.

"Dear Chapatti man, my paws are not as strong at swimming as I thought. Why don't you hop up between my ears?"

So that is just what the little chapatti did.

This time, the tiger swam so slow and low that the river splish-splashed around his neck and head.

"Friend Tiger, may I climb on to your nose?" squeaked the little chapatti. "The water is very near indeed."

"Do, my dear friend, do," said the tiger. "Roll up there right away. I hope my whiskers don't tickle you."

So that's just what the little chapatti did. He rolled right up on to the tiger's nose.

The little chapatti stood proudly, watching the river bank get closer.

"We're nearly there!" he cried.

Then, suddenly he noticed that the tiger's smile was much wider than before.

"Tiger?" he asked in a worried voice. "Why are you smiling so very, very much?"

"Ah, my dear little Chapatti Man," sighed the tiger. "Can't you guess? Well, it's like this ..."

Quickly, quickly, the tiger tossed up his head.

Flip-flap! Up flew the little chapatti, into the air.

Flip-flop! Down he tumbled, just as the tiger opened his jaws and closed them. Snap! Gulp!

That was the end of the bold little Chapatti Man.

So nobody – not the woman nor the cat nor the dog nor the goat nor the cow nor the elephant – knew what became of him. Nobody except that clever, cunning tiger – and YOU!

From **The Runaway Dinner** by Allan Ahlberg

One sunny summer's day, just as Banjo, with his knife in one hand and his fork in the other, was leaning forward and smiling happily at the thought of eating his dinner, the sausage – Melvin, his name was – jumped, yes, jumped, right up off the plate ... and ran away.

Well then, of course, as you might expect, the fork ran after the sausage, the knife ran after the fork, the plate ran after the knife, the little table and the little chair ran after the plate, and Banjo, that hungry little boy, ran after all of them.

Modern fiction

From **Tom's Sausage Lion** by Michael Morpurgo

It was Christmas Eve when Tom first saw the lion. His mother had sent him out to fetch the logs, and there was a lion padding through the orchard with a string of sausages hanging from its mouth. Tom ran back inside the house to tell them, but his father just laughed and his mother said he must have been imagining things. He told them and he told them, but they wouldn't even come out to look.

'But it's true,' Tom shouted. 'It was a real lion, I know it was.'

'Perhaps it just looked like a lion,' said his mother. 'After all it is getting dark outside, isn't it, dear?'

'It couldn't have been anything else,' Tom said. 'There's nothing else looks like a lion.' But they wouldn't listen.

'That's enough, Tom,' said his father who was already cross. 'It's Christmas Eve, not April Fool's Day. You don't really expect us to believe a story like that, do you? We're not that stupid, you know. I don't want to hear another word about it, hear me? Else I'll send you to your room, Christmas Eve or no Christmas Eve.'

'But it was a lion, a real lion,' said Tom. 'Honest.'

'Right that's it,' his father said banging the table and pointing to the door. 'Upstairs.'

...

When he got on the school bus that first morning he was longing to tell someone about his lion. He hardly waited till he sat down before he told them the whole story.

'Twice I seen him,' he said. 'Once with Mrs Blunden's sausages and once with the turkey. Massive he was. Got green eyes, at least I think they were green. And you should've seen his teeth – long as my fingers they were. He crushed those turkey bones like they were wafers.'

When he had finished he looked around at his friends. They were all open-mouthed. None of them said anything until Barry Parsons spoke up. Barry Parsons had never liked Tom, and Tom had never much liked him. Tom had taken his place as right back in the school football team and Barry had never forgiven him.

'Pull the other one, Tom,' said Barry. 'Aren't no lions around here.'

'Well I seen him,' Tom said, looking around at the others. He could see they didn't believe him either. 'It's true. I did.'

'Who else saw it then?' Barry asked.

'Just me,' Tom said quietly. 'Wasn't anyone else there. But I saw him right close up. Honest.'

'Then why didn't he eat you if you were that close?' Barry went on. 'S'pose you shook his paw and wished him a happy Christmas.' And then the others began to laugh.

...

It was five to nine and the playground was full of children when
they walked in through the gates with the lion between them.
It was rather like dropping a pebble in a pond. As they saw the
lion, the children moved slowly backwards to the railings around
the playground. One or two ran screaming into the school, but most
were quite silent. Tom and Clare stood beside the lion in the middle
of the empty playground. A few children whimpered and clung to
each other; but most just stared at the lion, paralysed with terror.

Tom looked round the playground until he found who he was
looking for. Barry Parsons was standing up against the wall
under the conker tree that leaned out over the playground.
Tom, Clare and the lion walked slowly towards him.

'He looks terrified,' said Clare.

'Yes he does,' said Tom, 'doesn't he?'

'Don't come any closer,' Barry shouted at them. 'Keep away. He'll kill me.'

'What will?' said Tom.

'That thing, that lion thing. Keep it away.' Barry was swallowing hard. His face had gone quite pale.

'But I thought you said I was making it all up about the lion, Barry,' Tom said. The lion sniffed at Barry's jeans and began to lick them. Barry closed his eyes. 'Looks as if he likes the taste of you, Barry,' said Tom. 'And he hasn't had his breakfast yet.'

Barry tried to edge away along the wall. 'Don't try and run away, Barry, else he'll eat you. Just keep quite still.' The lion looked up at Barry and licked his whiskers.

Nonsense poetry

The Owl and the Pussy-Cat

I

The Owl and the Pussy-Cat went to sea
In a beautiful pea-green boat,
They took some honey, and plenty of money,
Wrapped up in a five-pound note.
The Owl looked up to the stars above,
And sang to a small guitar,
"O lovely Pussy! O Pussy, my love,
"What a beautiful Pussy you are,
"You are,
"You are!
"What a beautiful Pussy you are!"

II

Pussy said to the Owl, "You elegant fowl!
"How charmingly sweet you sing!
"O let us be married! too long we have tarried:
"But what shall we do for a ring?"
They sailed away for a year and a day,
To the land where the Bong-Tree grows,
And there in a wood a Piggy-wig stood,
With a ring at the end of his nose,
His nose,
His nose,
With a ring at the end of his nose.

III

"Dear Pig, are you willing to sell for one shilling
"Your ring?" Said the Piggy, "I will."
So they took it away, and were married next day
By the Turkey who lives on the hill.
They dined on mince, and slices of quince,
Which they ate with a runcible spoon;
And hand in hand, on the edge of the sand,
They danced by the light of the moon,
The moon,
The moon,
They danced by the light of the moon.

Edward Lear

Nonsense poetry
From The Jumblies

They sailed away in a Sieve, they did,
In a Sieve they sailed so fast,
With only a beautiful pea-green veil
Tied with a riband by way of a sail,
To a small tobacco-pipe mast;
And every one said, who saw them go,
"Oh won't they be soon upset, you know!
For the sky is dark, and the voyage is long,
And happen what may, it's extremely wrong
In a Sieve to sail so fast!"
Far and few, far and few,
Are the lands where the Jumblies live;
Their heads are green, and their hands are blue,
And they went to sea in a Sieve.

...

Edward Lear

Descriptive poetry
Spin Me a Web, Spider

Spin me a web, spider,
Across the window-pane
For I shall never break it
And make you start again.

Cast your net of silver
As soon as it is spun,
And hang it with the morning dew
That glitters in the sun.

It's strung with pearls and diamonds,
The finest ever seen,
Fit for any royal King
Or any royal Queen.

Would you, could you, bring it down
In the dust to lie?
Any day of the week, my dear,
Said the nimble fly.

Charles Causley

Descriptive poetry
Who's There?

Knock, knock!
Who's there?
cried the spider.
Stand and wait!
But she knew by the
gentle tweak of the web
it was her mate.

Knock, knock!
Who's there?
cried the spider.
Call your name!
But she knew by the
soft tap-tap on the silk
her spiderlings came.

Knock, knock!
Who's there?
cried the spider.
Who goes by?
But she knew by the
shaking of her net
it was the fly.

Judith Nicholls

Whisky frisky,
Hipperty hop,
Up he goes,
To the tree top!

Whirly, twirly,
Round and round,
Down he scampers
To the ground.

Furly, curly,
What a tail,
Tall as a feather,
Broad as a sail.

Where's his supper?
In the shell.
Snappy, cracky,
Out it fell.

Anon.

Word-play poetry
Eletelephony

Once there was an elephant,
Who tried to use the telephant –
No! No! I mean an elephone
Who tried to use the telephone –
(Dear me! I am not certain quite
That even now I've got it right.)

Howe'er it was, he got his trunk
Entangled in the telephunk;
The more he tried to get it free,
The louder buzzed the telephee –
(I fear I'd better drop the song
Of elephop and telephong!)

Laura E. Richards

From **50 Science Things to Make and Do**
by Georgina Andrews and Kate Knighton

What grows best?

Find out what seeds need to grow well.

1. Take three plates and make a pile of ten kitchen towels on each one. Lay a pastry cutter on each pile.

2. Spoon water onto two of the plates to soak the towels. Write "dry" along one side of the pile without water.

3. Sprinkle cress seeds into each cutter. Hold the cutter and spread the seeds to the edges with your finger.

4. Carefully remove the cutters. Put one of the watered plates in a cupboard, and the other two near a window.

5. Every day, add water around the seeds on the "wet" plates, but don't pour water over the seeds.

6. After about a
week, some of the
seeds will have
grown into plants.
Which plates look
the healthiest?

What's going on?

The dry seeds don't grow at all, as seeds need water to sprout.
But, once they've sprouted, they need light to make food, so the
plants in the dark cupboard are yellow. The wet plate by the
window grows successfully, as it has both water and light.

From **Your Senses** by Sally Morgan

Hearing sounds

Sounds are all around you and you use your ears to hear them.

Sounds are made when something **vibrates**. For example, a guitar makes a sound when its strings are plucked.

Your ears collect the sounds and send them into a tube called an ear canal. They reach your eardrum and make it vibrate. The vibrations pass to your cochlea. This is a fluid-filled tube that is coiled just like a snail's shell. Inside your cochlea, the liquid moves tiny hairs that send messages along nerves to your brain. Your brain works out what the sounds are and where they came from.

Your ear

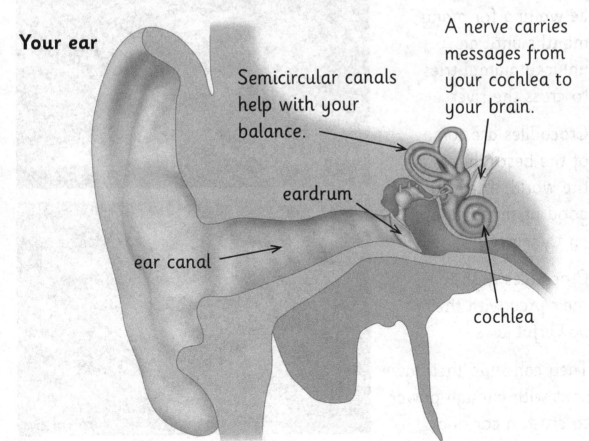

Semicircular canals help with your balance.

A nerve carries messages from your cochlea to your brain.

eardrum

ear canal

cochlea

Explanation texts

From **Living Dinosaurs** by Jonathan and Angela Scott

Crocodiles today

In Africa, herds of animals cross the River Mara each year, looking for fresh grass to eat. **Nile crocodiles** lie in wait for them.

Large crocodiles only need a few big meals a year. The rest of the time they mostly eat fish. Some crocodiles lie waiting for many months until an unlucky animal tries to cross the river.

Crocodiles are some of the best hunters in the world. They are good at sneaking up on their **prey**.

Crocodiles grab their prey with their powerful jaws.

They can snap their jaws shut with enough power to crush a car door.

Eyes, nostrils and ears are on top of their heads, so they can swim without being seen.

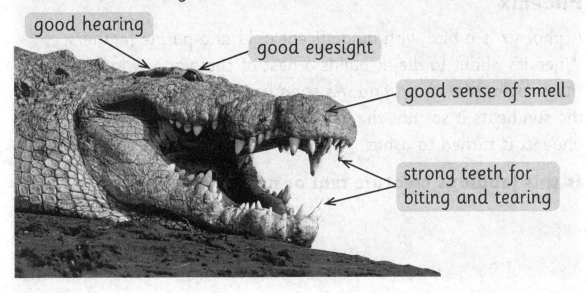

good hearing

good eyesight

good sense of smell

strong teeth for biting and tearing

Crocodiles catch their prey and try to drown it by pulling it underwater. Crocodiles have a flap of skin to stop water going down their throats, so they can go underwater with their mouths open.

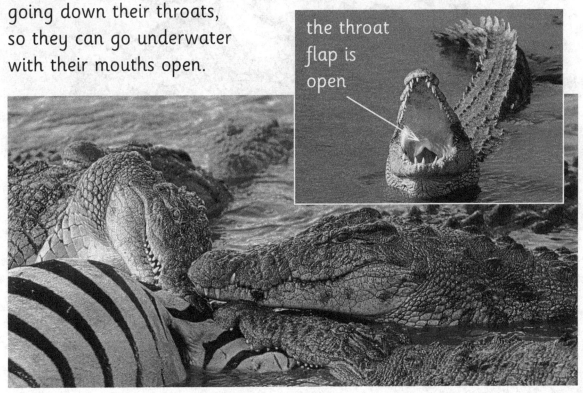

the throat flap is open

From **Fabulous Creatures – Are They Real?**
by Scoular Anderson

Phoenix

A phoenix is a bird with magnificent gold and purple feathers. When it's about to die, it builds a nest of cinnamon twigs in the tallest palm tree it can find. As soon as it jumps into the nest, the sun heats it so that the nest bursts into flames and the phoenix is turned to ashes.

Is this fabulous creature real or not?

No!

The phoenix is a bird from an ancient Egyptian legend. People believed that the bird lived for a long time – between 500 and 1,000 years. It never ate anything – ever!

In the legend, as soon as the phoenix and its nest had been burnt, a small worm crawled out of the ashes. This eventually turned into another phoenix – so the bird never really died.

The word "phoenix" is Greek, meaning "palm tree" or "purple".

In Egypt, the phoenix was known as the Bennu bird. When someone talks about something "rising like a phoenix from the ashes", they mean it has been reborn.

41

From **Gerbils** by Laura Howell

What is a gerbil?

Gerbils are small, mouse-like animals with hairy tails and strong back legs. They are clean, fun-loving and make excellent pets. This book will tell you what you need to know about buying and taking care of your first gerbil.

Appearance

Gerbils are about 10cm (4in) tall – larger than a mouse, but smaller than a rat.

Although it's hard to tell here, a gerbil's tail is as long as its body. It helps the gerbil to balance.

Long, sensitive whiskers

Sharp claws for digging

Powerful back legs for jumping

Desert diggers

Wild gerbils and their relatives come from desert regions.
They live in groups called colonies, inside huge networks
of tunnels that they dig in the sand

The entrance to a gerbil's
tunnel is only big enough to let
a gerbil through. Most enemies
are too big to fit.

Need to gnaw

Like rats and hamsters, gerbils are rodents. These are animals
with two pairs of strong front teeth for gnawing. The name
"gerbil" comes from the Arabic word "jarbu", meaning "rodent".

Gerbils and other
rodents gnaw
things to keep
their teeth from
growing too long.

From **Diary of a Fly** by Doreen Cronin

JUNE 7

Tomorrow is the first day of school. I'm so nervous. What if I'm the only one that eats regurgitated food?

JUNE 8

Great news! Everyone eats regurgitated food!

...

JUNE 14

Today we practised landing on moving targets.

I am standing on her head right now.

AUGUST 1

I just know I would make an excellent superhero:
I have 4,000 lenses in each eye.
I can walk on walls.
I can change direction in flight
faster than the blink of a
human eye.

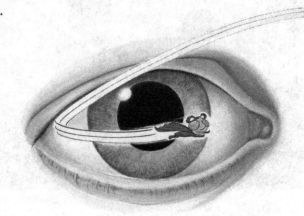

Spider said, "Superheroes save the world from outer-space villains. Your brain is the size of a sesame seed."

I never thought about it that way.

AUGUST 2

Today I told Worm and Spider that I could never be a superhero like I wanted.

Worm looked me right in the eyes and said, "The world needs all kinds of heroes."

Spider said, "I never thought about it that way."

Neither did I.

Diary recounts

From **Diary of a Worm** by Doreen Cronin

MARCH 29

Today I tried to teach Spider how to dig.

First of all his legs got stuck.

Then he swallowed a load of dirt.

Tomorrow he's going to teach me how to walk upside down.

...

JULY 4

When I grow up I want to be a Secret Service agent. Spider says I will have to be very careful because the prime minister might step on me by mistake.

"It's a dangerous job," I told him. "But someone's got to do it."

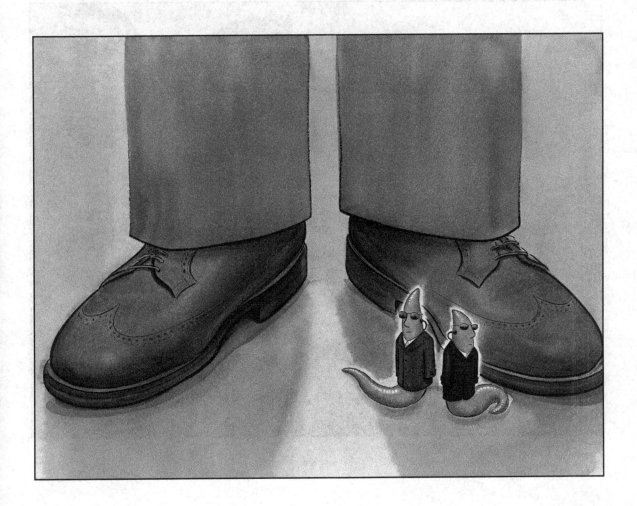

...

AUGUST 1

It's not always easy being a worm. We're very small and sometimes people forget that we're even here.

But, like Mum always says, the earth never forgets we're here.

Fantasy fiction

From **The Incredible Book Eating Boy** by Oliver Jeffers

Henry loved BOOKS.
But not like you and I love books, no.
Not quite …

… Henry loved to EAT books.

It all began quite by mistake one afternoon when
he wasn't paying attention.

He wasn't sure at first, and tried eating a single
word, just to test.

Next, he tried a whole sentence and then the
whole page.

Yes, Henry definitely liked them. By Wednesday,
he had eaten a WHOLE book.

And by the end of the month he could eat a whole
book in one go.

Henry loved eating all sorts of books.
Story books, dictionaries, atlases,
joke books, books of facts, even maths
books. But red ones were his favourite.

But here is the best bit:

The more he ate, the smarter he got.

...

But then things started going not
quite so well.

In fact, they started going very, very,
wrong. Henry was eating too many
books, and too quickly at that.

He was beginning to feel a little ill.

...

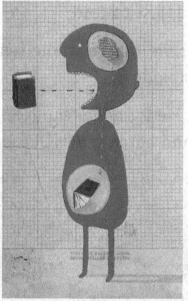

Then, after a while, and almost by
accident, Henry picked up a half-eaten
book from the floor. But instead of
putting it in his mouth ...
Henry opened it up ...

... and began to read.

And it was SO good.

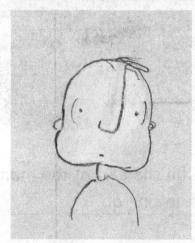

Henry discovered that he loved to read. And he
thought that if he read enough he might still
become the smartest person on Earth.
It would just take a bit longer.

Now Henry reads all the time ...
although every now and then ...

From **Black Dog** by Levi Pinfold

One day, a black dog came to visit the Hope family.
Mr Hope was the first see it.

"My goodness!" he cried, dropping his toast. He didn't waste
any time in phoning the police.

"There's a black dog the size of a tiger outside my house!" he told
the policeman.

The policeman laughed.

"What should I do?" asked Mr Hope.

"Don't go outside," said the policeman, and put down the phone.

Mrs Hope was next to get up.

"My goodness!" she cried, dropping her mug of tea.
She didn't waste any time in calling for Mr Hope.

"Did you know there's a black dog the size of an elephant outside?"
she yelled.

"Yes," said Mr Hope.

"What should we do?" asked Mrs Hope.

"Turn out the lights so it doesn't know we're here!"

It was then that the youngest member of the Hope family, called
Small (for short), noticed that there was something going on.

"What are you lot doing under there?"

"We're hiding from the Black Dog!" they whispered.

"Oh, you are such sillies," said Small, opening the front door.

"Don't go out there!" gasped her family.

"The hound will eat you up!"

"It'll munch your head!"

"It'll crunch your bones!"

But Small had gone anyway.

...

"All right then," she said. "If you're going to eat me, you'll have to catch me first." And with that she scurried into the lowering trees. As she ran, she made up a song:

"You can't follow where I go, unless you shrink, or don't you know?"

The Black Dog followed ...

Next she scuttled through the playground, down the slide and around the roundabout, singing:

"You've a BIG TUM, I'm all slim, you'll fit through if you're more trim."

And still the Black Dog followed …

…

Finally, Small had run all the way back to the house.

"You'll find out why they all hide, if you follow me inside."

And with that, Small tumbled into her warm home through the cat flap. She really was that small.

And so, by now, was the Black Dog.

Inside, Small grabbed a washing basket and, as the Black Dog scrabbled in behind her, she covered him with a loud "HA!"

Just then, the rest of the Hope family popped up from behind their barricade.

"You haven't been munched!" cried Mrs Hope.

"You haven't been eaten!" yelled Maurice Hope (missing a poetic opportunity).

"But where's the Black Dog?" asked Adeline.

Without a word, Small lifted the basket.

Letters

From **The Day the Crayons Quit** by Drew Daywalt

Dear Duncan,

I'm tired off being called "light brown" or "dark tan" because I am neither.

I am BEIGE and I am proud. I'm also tired of being second place to Mr Brown Crayon.

It's not fair that Brown gets all the bears, ponies and puppies while the only things I get are turkey dinners (if I'm lucky) and wheat, and let's be honest - when was the last time you saw a kid excited about colouring wheat?

Your BEIGE friend,

Beige Crayon

Dear Duncan,

As Green Crayon, I am writing for two reasons.
One is to say I like my work - loads of crocodiles,
trees, dinosaurs and frogs. I have no problems and
wish to congratulate you on a very successful
"colouring things green" career so far.

The second reason I write is for my friends,
Yellow Crayon and Orange Crayon, who are no longer
speaking to each other. Both crayons feel THEY should
be the colour of the sun.

Please settle this soon because they're driving the
rest of us CRAZY!

Your happy friend,

Green Crayon

Letters

From **Dear Greenpeace** by Simon James

Dear Greenpeace,

I am now putting salt into the pond every day before
school and last night I saw my whale smile. I think
he is feeling better. Do you think he might be lost?

Love,

Emily

Dear Emily,

Please don't put any more salt in the pond,
I'm sure your parents won't be pleased.

I'm afraid there can't be a whale in your pond,
because whales don't get lost, they always know
where they are in the oceans.

Yours sincerely,

Greenpeace

From **Antarctica – Land of the Penguins**
by Jonathan and Angela Scott

What is Antarctica?

Antarctica is that magical land at the far south of the world. It's so wild and beautiful that it's hard to describe what it feels like to be there.

It is the coldest, windiest place on Earth, with temperatures as low as -89°C (-129°F). The Southern Ocean that surrounds it has larger waves and stronger winds than anywhere else on Earth.

It seems hard to believe that anything could live in such a place. However, one kind of bird survives there in large numbers — the penguin.

The Antarctic mainland is enormous. It is 58 times larger than the United Kingdom. In winter it doubles in size, as the sea around it freezes.

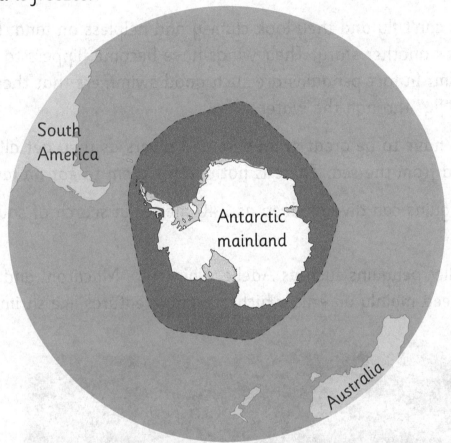

South America

Antarctic mainland

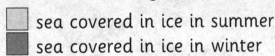

The area of the Antarctic nearly doubles in size in winter.

☐ sea covered in ice in summer
☐ sea covered in ice in winter

Most creatures can't survive inland during the winter. Some live on the coasts which are warmer but most move further north to escape the extreme cold. The Emperor penguin is one of the few creatures which can cope during these dark and freezing months.

How penguins survive

Great swimmers

Penguins can't fly and they look clumsy and helpless on land, but in the sea it's another story. Their wings have become flippers to help them swim. In fact penguins are such good swimmers that they seem to "fly" through the water.

Penguins have to be great swimmers and divers as they get all of their food from the sea. There is nothing for them to eat on land.

King penguins can dive as deep as 240 metres in search of squid and fish.

The smaller penguins such as Adelie, Chinstrap, Macaroni and Gentoo feed mainly on krill, which are tiny creatures like shrimps.

Keeping warm

Penguins have feathers to keep them warm, just like a duvet keeps you warm in bed. They also have a thick layer of fat beneath their skin for the same reason. This fat layer is called blubber. Whales and seals also have blubber to keep them warm.

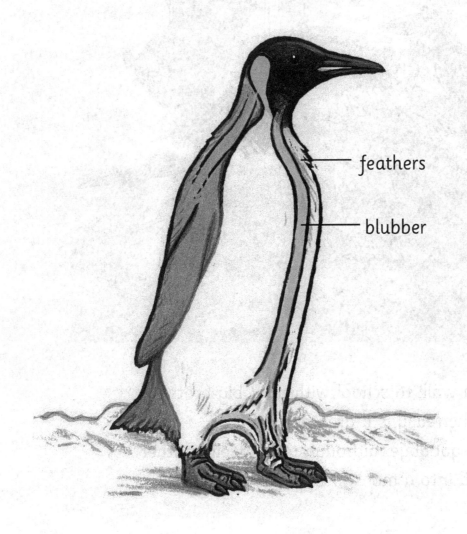

feathers

blubber

Longer poems

If

If you can keep your head when alligators
are stealing all the bedclothes from your bed
and keep your cool when, 15 minutes later,
a greedy hippo eats your eggy bread ...

If you can walk to school with your big brother
although he really is a dreadful sight,
and wave goodbye, although your lovely mother
has turned into a monster overnight ...

If you can cross the playground in the morning –
a playground full of fearsome dinosaurs –
and keep on walking when, without a warning,
they raise their heads and roar and roar and roar ...

If you can grin and bear it when your teacher,
who really is a dragon through and through,
tells you to sit beside a toothy creature
who must have just escaped from Scary Zoo ...

If you can lend your ruler – though he chews it –
if you can let him use your felt-tip pens,
if you can lend a hand – although he'll bruise it –
and treat him just like any other friend ...

If you can eat the food served up by mummies
with trolls and lizards in the dinner hall,
and when the others groan and hold their tummies
say, "Actually, that wasn't bad at all ..."

If you can stand and watch a spaceship landing
and when the others run away in fright,
you treat the strange green men with understanding
and though they're rude, you are still polite ...

If you can count to ten while angry rhinos
are grunting (just because they can't do sums)
and say, "I'll teach you everything that I know
but quick – before the dragon teacher comes ..."

And then, if you can play your new recorder
up there, on stage — you're feeling rather stressed
— and all around there's panic and disorder
but you still try to do your very best ...

If you can play at baseball with a cheetah
who, fast as lightning, runs from base to base
and even though you know you'll never beat her,
you somehow keep a smile on your face,

If you can run, though others can run faster,
and cheer the winner, "Hip-hip-hip hooray!"
if you can try to stop a near-disaster,
although you'd really rather run away ...

If you can keep your head when all about you
are losing theirs and blaming it on you,
if you can let them fight it out without you,
if everyone's a monster, but not you ...

If you then meet a tearful pirate fairy
and kindly help her up from off the ground
and wonder how the world can be this scary
and stop and think ... and turn ... and look around ...

Then you will see that they're just human beings
with hopes and worries much the same as you.
despite their snatch and grab and disagreeing
there's lots of lovely things they also do.

If you can see all this and never doubt it
(though crocodiles will eat your cheesy snack)
you'll love this world and everything about it
and – what is more – the world will love you back.

Everyone's a monster
We're all human beings

Mij Kelly